A Journey of Pain and Peace:
Learning from Loss

Carolyn DeArmond Blevins

FirstXaris Books

A Journey of Pain and Peace: Learning from Loss
ISBN: Softcover
Copyright © 2024 by Carolyn DeArmond Blevins

First edition published in 2012.

FirstXaris Books is an imprint of Parson's Porch *&* Company (PP*&*C) in Cleveland, Tennessee. PP*&*C is a self-funded charity which earns money by publishing books of noted authors, representing all genres. Its face and voice is **David Russell Tullock** who you can contact at: dtullock@parsonsporch.com.

Parson's Porch *&* Company *turns books into bread & milk* by sharing its profits with the poor.

www.parsonsporch.com

A Journey of Pain and Peace:
Learning from Loss

Dedicated to

Kym
who brought me so much joy for 32 years

Bill, Suzanne, Art, and Alan and Shannon
who travel this journey with me

Alex, Jaclyn, Sydney and Noah
who had to deal with loss so early

Many friends
who care deeply and teach me so much

Contents

Foreword

Preface

W alking helps! Walking is therapy for me. When I walk I think; I sort; I get in touch with my anger; I relive my pain as a way of coming to terms with it; I process. I do some of my best thinking when I walk. Often something that I am dealing with is much clearer when I return from a walk.

Much of this book was born as I walked in our neighborhood. I relived the pain. I relived the compassion. I struggled with loss. I tried to sort out how I live with this loss. I prayed. Thoughts about pain, loss, and peace became clearer as I walked. Heading to the computer as I entered the house to jot down those thoughts was a typical experience. Perhaps it is appropriate that a book about a personal journey was significantly birthed as I walked.

Walking is therapy for me. So is reading. A few months after our daughter Kym's death, I began to search for books to guide me on this new journey. Many good books by others who had walked similar journeys or by professional grief counselors stimulated and comforted me. I learned so much from them. Writing about what I learned became another avenue of healing. Walking, reading and writing pave the path of this journey.

What a Day!

Death is hardest to comprehend without any forewarning.

Elisabeth Kubler-Ross and David Kessler in *On Grief and Grieving: Finding the Meaning of Grief Through the Five Stages of Loss:*[1]

Y ou never know when you put your feet on the floor in the morning what that day will bring." How many times have I said that over the years?

When I put my feet on the floor on Saturday, August 28, 2004, I expected a full day. Earlier that week my mother-in-law died and this day relatives would arrive for lunch after which we would have the visitation,

---

[1] Elizabeth Kubler-Ross and David Kessler, *On Grief and Grieving: Finding the Meaning of Grief Through the Five Stages of Loss,* (New York, Scribner, 2005), 195.

funeral and burial. As I returned from an early morning walk my husband Bill said that the local retirement home where my mother lived, called saying that she was hemorrhaging. Soon I was following the ambulance to the emergency room and standing by as she was settled into an examining room. My brother Ray, who lives in another state, was on his way to pick up Mother and take her to the funeral. I reached him by phone, alerting him to her presence in ER rather than the retirement home. About 11:00 he arrived at the hospital, and I dashed home to get dressed and set out the food the church folks brought for the relatives who gathered at our house.

As I curled my hair Alan, our youngest son, came in asking if Kym, our youngest daughter, was planning to come for lunch. A single 32-year-old, she lived about five minutes away in her own home. I assured him she was. Because she did not answer either her land phone or cell phone and did not come to the door when he went over there, he was concerned. I suggested that he break in through a window, that something was wrong. She was sick or had fallen and needed help. It never occurred to me to think of anything worse than that. As he got a ladder from the garage our older son Art agreed to go with him.

Stirring sugar into the tea in the kitchen a few minutes later, I heard the phone ring. Bill answered it. The next thing I knew he was standing in the kitchen saying, "Carolyn, Kym is dead!" Those are the three most knee-buckling, heart-crushing words I have ever heard. I broke into loud sobs as he held me in his arms. No! No! No! That was unimaginable. Kym

14

dead? Not Kym! She was only 32 years old. In fine health. This could not be! I sobbed loudly and uncontrollably. Relatives came from the living room thinking that my mother must have died and were shocked to learn that it was Kym. The phone call was from Alan who had crawled in Kym's open bedroom window and found her dead in the bed. He ran to the front door and let Art in, then called home. When Bill answered and heard the news, he told Alan to call the police immediately. Within minutes Bill and I were on our way to Kym's house.

No parent wants to drive up to her child's home and see a fire truck, an ambulance and a police car, but that is what we saw. Policemen were on the front porch. Kym's death appeared to be a homicide! Kym's death was shocking enough, but murder? Who would want to kill Kym? And why? And what was the cause of death? We had a million questions. Alan and Art walked around in shock, as did we. Immediately I told the policeman that I wanted to go inside, that I would not bother anything, I just wanted to put my arms around her body and tell her that I loved her. He said I could not. I begged. He was kind but firm, a man who no doubt had dealt with frantic mothers many times. Several times over the next hour I begged to go in. Each time I was firmly and politely refused. Then I began asking for some information— any little bit of information, please. Again, patiently and firmly I was told they could not give me any information. Once when I was begging, I saw Art standing to the side and knew he must be embarrassed by my begging, so I said, "I know I am embarrassing my children, but that's OK because they have embarrassed me at times, too." My heaviness needed a little levity apparently.

The feeling of knowing that my daughter's body was on the other side of that wall and that I could not go to it was extraordinarily painful. I cannot describe that pain adequately. A wall and a policeman stood between me and the daughter I loved. Emotion, not reason, was my mode. Of course, I know that the scene of an unnatural death must be left undisturbed. Of course, I know that I could do nothing for her at that point. Of course I know that my going in would have been for me and not for her. But I was not into reason; I was operating on high emotion mode, and I wanted to be with Kym. The authorities wouldn't let me. So I sat in a lawn chair on the front porch with a friend and sobbed. I simply could not bear the pain. "Loss and helplessness are the two most painful experiences that human beings have to bear" says Barbara Rosof[2] and feeling helpless is a keen part of loss. I was overwhelmed by both. My loss intensified my helplessness. My helplessness intensified my loss.

For almost two hours while our out-of-town relatives at home took care of the lunch, Bill and I waited with emergency personnel for the arrival of a lab team from the Tennessee Bureau of Investigation. Getting those men from a nearby city on a weekend was not a quick process. In the meantime, friends and ministers from our church arrived with long hugs and caring words. Our

---

[2] Barbara D. Rosof, *The Worst Loss: How Families Heal from the Death of a Child,* (New York: Henry Holt & Co, 1994), xi.

oldest daughter Suzanne arrived with her two children, Jaclyn, 13 and Noah, 9, who were quite traumatized by the news. Kym had lived with them for several months when she first moved to Atlanta. We cried. We waited.

As the one o'clock hour approached, the time of visitation prior to his mother's funeral, Bill concluded that there would be no way we could emotionally go through that important ritual. A friend and our ministers volunteered to go to the funeral home, greet those who came and explain why we would be there for the funeral but not the visitation. (Since that day I have often wondered what it must have been like for our friends, who arrived for the funeral of a grandmother, to learn of the tragic death of her granddaughter. What a shock that must have been.) We hoped that by the time of the funeral we would have seen the TBI personnel arrive. Shortly before 2:00 we realized that would not happen, left this home that now was the temporary tomb of our daughter and went to the funeral of Bill's mother.

As we sat in a back room of a funeral home, my physician and neighbor came in and asked if I would like him to prescribe some medication for me, some for day and some for night. I replied that I would take the days as they came but wanted to sleep at night. As our children and our daughter-in-law, Shannon, gathered in that room we realized that we would be back here in a day or two planning Kym's funeral. We couldn't believe that reality. At Bill's request there were minor changes made in his mother's funeral in light of our new trauma.

At that service we sat as a family for the first time without Kym. We sat there trying to focus on grandmother's death while still in shock over Kym's. Surely our friends were having similar difficulties. As we rode to the cemetery I was crying again and telling Bill of changes in my own burial plans. For years I instructed my family to cremate my body and sprinkle my ashes in Cades Cove in the Great Smoky Mountains, a most serene and beautiful place. But on this day those plans became history. I now made it clear that I wanted my ashes buried beside Kym, a plan that had never crossed my mind before this day. As we sat at the cemetery before the grave, I could only think of doing this again very soon. My grieving of family deaths was already mixed up and could not easily be sorted.

Returning home I realized that when I put my feet on the floor that morning, I did not know that in addition to a funeral, I would be in ER with my mother, and mourning the tragic death of Kym. And now we waited for the officers from the local sheriff's department and the TBI to come to our home and interview our family. What a day!

Morning and evening were the first day—of life without Kym.

A Gift Stolen

Before July 31, 1973 our family of five had no Kym. In the early seventies as we contemplated adding a fourth child to our family, our oldest child, ten-year-old Suzanne, heard our discussion. She promptly declared that if we had another baby it had better be a girl. She thought that two brothers, Art, 8 and Alan 3, were enough for any girl! We assured her that we had no control over what the gender would be. But her request (or edict!) and the fact that in the early seventies there was an emphasis on zero population growth caused us to rethink our plan. Rather than add another child to the world's population, why not adopt one who was already here and needed a home? And that is the reason that on July 31, 1973, we stood at the window in Chicago's O'Hare Airport and watched that huge Northwest Orient 747 from Seoul, Korea glide down from the skies bringing our new Korean daughter. In a few very long impatient moments a charming 15-month-old we would name Kym, was in our arms and in our hearts. Thirty-one years later she glided up the stairs from our basement family room and within hours was taken from our arms but not our hearts.

In between those two life-changing events, she blossomed as a charming, independent-minded, beautiful young woman who hated looking different but worked diligently to be different in her own way. As one of her dear friends said, "She liked to be seen, but not disturbed!" Just eight months before her death she had purchased her own home. Two months before her life was taken she had the Lasik surgery she had wanted for some time. It seemed to be good period in her short life. The love of her life had just gone with his National Guard unit to Mississippi to train for its tour in Iraq and they made plans for his return.

But in August 2004 she was taken from us. As a result, we are changed people-all five of us. The minutes, hours, days, weeks, and years since that day have been a journey we never anticipated, and no family wants to take. As is true of many painful experiences we have learned so much.

Brook Noel and Pamela D. Blair expressed the life-changing news so well: ". . . in a split-second with the news of a loved one's sudden death, the world changes forever. . .. No time for preparation. No time to gather what we'll need for our journey. No time for finished business or goodbyes. . .. After the news of sudden death, we awake less whole with a gaping hole left by the death of the person we loved."[3] *Now our journey was to discover how we would live with that hole.*

What a day! On the first day of a journey a stranger forced us to take. Like a bolt of lightning, we were knocked into a pit of pain. We began to make our way through this pit of grief and pain and eventually to find paths of peace.

> . . .*this savage journey requires leaving what we know behind and becoming open, and truly vulnerable, to the truth about living a human life. We must bear the pain, endure the excruciating moments that declare with their arrival: "Life will never be the same."*
>
> *Kathleen Brehony in After the Darkest Hour: How Suffering Begins the Journey to Wisdom.*[4]

---

[4] Kathleen A. Brehony, *After the Darkest Hour: How Suffering Begins the Journey to Wisdom,* (Henry Holt & Co., 2000), 78.

The Power of Hugs

No one should carry this terrible burden alone. Even the strongest among us asks for help along the way. We fall, and someone helps us until we are strong enough to begin again.

Kathleen O'Hara in *A Grief Like No Other: Surviving the Violent Death of Someone You Love*[5]

My brain, heart, body and soul needed the break that the sleep medication provided that night. Four hours of sleep is better than none, so I lay in bed in the wee morning hours trying to come to terms with the new realities of the day before. I did

---

[5] Kathleen O'Hara, *A Grief Like No Other: Surviving the Violent Death of Someone You Love*, (New York, Marlowe and Co., 2006, 51.

not know how to do this—say a final goodbye to a child.

My reactions the day before made it clear that I was not in a rational state of mind. I could only take this uncharted journey one emotional step at a time. On this day and the days that followed I cried on many shoulders and said repeatedly, "this is so hard." When my body is wounded, the wound is treated. Some new tissue grows in the wounded area. Eventually new skin covers the previous wound. If the wound is deep, a scar remains. A lot of healing has occurred, but the body is forever scarred. Over the next months and years after Kym's death I discovered that my wounded spirit would also heal. There was new growth in that deep wound. But the scar is there forever.

One by one I discovered the compassionate and healing power of hugs. I don't remember what individuals said although their words told me clearly that they cared, but I felt the hugs. When my world seemed shattered, two arms wrapped around my broken being, assuring me that another person shared my sorrow.

Our granddaughters from Denver, Alex 13 and Sydney 10 arrived the next day with the hugs we were waiting for. There was so much grief in our family.

People hugged me and I them. Some of these people I would not have dreamed of hugging before August 28th! Now I was glad to feel their arms around me as I held on to them. The physical contact of arms around my aching being, the emotional empathy of a person who cared that I was hurting, and the shoulder to lay my head on, combined to make a hug feel like a welcome, temporary cocoon of shelter.

How many times have I wondered what to say to a person whose heart was broken over what life had tossed them? Now I know that my words may be helpful, but my hug conveys more than my tongue can. A bear hug, an arm around the shoulder, a half hug—whatever a person was most comfortable with—said "I care" in a way that lovingly embraced me at a crucial point in my life. I heard the worst words I have ever heard and immediately I discovered the arms of Bill. Quickly other hugs followed. Hugs continued for days and even years. Caring, healing hugs.

Hugs come in various forms.
Caring voices on the other end of a telephone call brought the feeling of a verbal hug. Written hugs floated off cards as we opened them to find words that shared our pain and loss. "I hear your silent screams and it breaks my heart." "I remember. I care. I continue to pray." "We wish we could somehow soothe the hurt." "We pray that all of us who love you may absorb some of your pain." Emails quickly sent to say that someone remembered and cared about were technological hugs. Flowers were hugs of beauty. The dish of food was a culinary hug.

The night of the memorial service for Kym, a friend slipped a small bag into Bill's hand. When we got home we discovered she had given us a prescription for healing: a collection of prayers tied to scripture passages tightly rolled and insert in prescription bottles. Each passage had our names inserted. Each day we began the day by unrolling one and reading it together. When we read a prayer such as "Lord we ask for peace for Carolyn and Bill; Your peace, not the world's version. Comfort their hearts when they are troubled or fearful (John 14:27)" we felt a holy hug from our friend and God.

Kathleen Brehony says that in difficult times relationships of family and friends are like a container. They hold us together, enclosing us in a space filled with love and belonging. "Community is not a luxury. It's like air for us," she concludes[6.]

Friends and family were our container, holding us together. The sense of love and belonging as expressed in the variety of hugs was indeed air for our family.

> *This quest for belonging. . .is the deep, resonating sense that we are part of a group that surrounds us and holds us with love.*
>
> Kathleen Behoney in After the Darkest Hour: How Suffering Begins the Journey to Wisdom.[7]

---

[6] Brehony, 211

[7] Brehony, 209

This is So Hard

This is so hard." Those four words were repeated often on the shoulder and in the arms of friends over the next days and weeks. I knew of no other way to express how I felt. Later I read Kathleen Brehony's phrase: "a grief so deep it had no bottom."[9] That phrase explained why "this is so hard." The grief was

---

[8] Noel and Blair, 12

[9] Brehoney, 156

so deep. Rather early in my journey I found new words to explain my emotions: "I feel like I have been hit by a bomb that keeps on dropping."

The first and overwhelming feeling was that this experience was so very hard. "Hard" for me had a double meaning. Losing a daughter, my child, had not entered my mind, although every parent knows it is a possibility. Losing a child is so very hard. Knowing that some person on this earth deliberately took her life was simply beyond my imagination, but it was a fact with which I had to come to terms. Another "hard." This is so very hard. The bomb seemed to be in a slow drop that would not end. There was no bottom to it. My world and my family's world were turned upside down, inside out, and were very raw. Nothing was the same nor will ever be. Thirty-one years of family life with Kym was abruptly and cruelly ended. There is a hard line drawn now in our family's story: the time before Kym died and the time since Kym died. How in the world do I handle this reality?

"Hard" was the simple explanation for every aspect of my life at this time it seemed.

This is so hard—to be so sad.
Of course, I knew what sadness was. I thought when my father died or when our older children went through divorces that I knew what sadness was. And I did. But now I discovered new depths of sadness. The sadness seemed to permeate every bone in my body, every muscle, every cell, every crevice in my brain. It wrapped around me and through me. Never had I experienced such deep sadness.

As I was dealing with the new depths, I was also experiencing sudden waves of sadness, sometimes seeming to come out of nowhere, totally unexpected or predicted. I could go from feeling pretty good to feeling enormously sad in mere seconds. I had no idea what caused the swing and learned that nothing in particular caused it. It was an experience of grief. I began to compare it to an ocean. At times I floated in calm waters, calm with numbness, sometimes with a strange and brief peace. Then a huge wave of raw emotion swelled up and knocked me off my feet. Or a medium wave came and left me tearful. Or an undertow carried me sadly back into the ocean of grief. As a person who was able to control myself rather well most of the time, this inability to control this powerful emotion was quite disconcerting.

This is so hard. In the midst of my deep sadness I am learning that I am vulnerable, very vulnerable in grief.

This is so hard— to sleep.
Only medication gave me the relief of rest and temporary amnesia of my loss. It was a drugged sleep—not the best rest, but better than sleepless nights. I had never needed sleep assistance. But this was so hard, my mind could not shut down and my body could not relax. Each night I gladly and eagerly reached for the numbness that tiny pill would bring to my mind so my body could rest. I learned that if I wanted the physical and emotional strength for the next day I had to rely on medication at night to give me the rest I needed to have that strength.

This is hard—for our family.

The sudden and tragic death of Kym was hard for all of us: Bill, Suzanne, and especially our sons, Art and Alan who had discovered Kym's body and were dealing with frequent nightmares; Shannon, Alan's wife, who shared many of Kym's interests; Kym's beloved friend, who had to return to base. It was hard for each of us. It was hard for Kym's young nieces and nephew. Our children's former spouses had a hard time as well.

One evil act rained like an endless hailstorm on all of our family. Each of us was dealing with our own pain and trying to "be there" for other family members who were struggling also. As a mother and wife my natural instinct is to do all I can to heal the hurt when I see my family hurting. But how do I help others who are hurting when I have so much pain myself? We soon realized that while all of us went through similar stages of grief, we did not go through them at the same time, in the same order, or stay in that stage the same amount of time. That proved to be both beneficial at times and problematic at times. This is so hard.

This is so hard—to be a daughter.

For sixteen years since the death of my father I had been the child nearest to our mother and so had looked after her as she needed it. For five years she had lived in a retirement home in my hometown and I became more involved in her daily life and needs. The last three years she had a series of health problems that required more attention from me. Instead of going to the funeral that day in August as she had planned, Mother wound up in the hospital for a week. Instead of my brother and his wife coming in for a day to a funeral, they wound up staying a week while Mother was in the hospital and I, the daughter, was not very useful.

But when she was released from the hospital, life was not the same for her. Now in declining health, within one week she had lost her good friend Margaret (Bill's mother) and her granddaughter, Kym. She needed me now more than ever. Unfortunately, at this time it was so hard for me to be the daughter she needed. Now she needed a daughter who was not distracted by her own grief to walk with her through her own valley of decline and grief. I did my best, but it was so hard for me, an emotional cripple myself, to be there for her. Later it was of some comfort to me to find Barbara Rosof admitting: "When you cannot function at the level you usually expect of yourself, it hurts. . . The fact is that for now you are inadequate."[10] The more I read the more I was assured that feeling helpless is a part of the grief journey. On top of my grief or because of it, I faced a humbling reality: I am not superhuman; I have limits; I am inadequate. It was a hard lesson for me to learn when Mother needed me so much.

This is so hard—to be in public.
For three weeks I did not go to the store, Bill had less trouble with that, so he went for us. Although church

---

[10] Rosof, 244

was very important to me, I could not go to church. The thought of singing hymns and seeing people was too hard for me. Carolyn, the person who liked to be with people, was suddenly retreating from people. People were not the problem; I was. I felt so fragile emotionally that I had no confidence in handling myself publicly. It was too hard I thought, so I retreated into the privacy of our home where I felt safer emotionally.

This is so hard—to function.

A week or so after returning to teaching at Carson-Newman College I went to class one day and discovered that only three people in the class had read the material and come to class prepared. It was a critical moment for me. I stood there silently saying to myself that it was so hard for me to just get up, come to work, and teach this class, and yet they were not even bothering to read the material. I was really ticked. I did not want to use my own tragedy to lay guilt on them, but I did want them to prepare. So I dismissed the class and told them not to return and place their bodies in those seats until they had read. Then I left the room. I went to my office, shut the door, and lay down on the floor to get my act together before my next class. It was hard to function those days. (The next time that class met, those students were so well read. It was our best class session that term!)

This is so hard—to care about things that used to matter so much.

Responsibilities at home, at work, at church, or in civic organizations in one brief moment had paled in importance. Things that mattered so much to me just last week, I cared nothing about now. Obviously, I had to reconnect with things that matter but it would take a while to heal myself enough to care about matters beyond me. In the meantime, it was hard to really care about a lot of interests, activities, commitments, and responsibilities. When I returned to work I sat in important committee meetings thinking that what we were doing was not as important as I used to think. It was hard at times to remember that these things did matter. Eventually I got past such a negative view of the rest of life, but I learned: When others are going through difficult times, I need to give them time to return to the world that matters.

This is so hard---for church and college folks.
It was hard for our church family who ministered to us so well. One family in their church family was hurting and they were hurt too. It was hard for our college community. Within the first week of school, this small college community learned of three deaths: a student had been grabbed and killed in a foreign country while visiting her family before returning for the fall semester; our daughter was murdered; and a beloved retired professor died suddenly of a heart attack. Three tragedies the first week of the fall term. What a way to begin the year for these young people! Two of the deaths were young adults killed tragically and so death came too close for comfort for many of the students.

This is so hard—for families in our community.
Parents could not imagine losing a child, but this

death made that possibility more real. In this small college town, we felt rather isolated from the violent crimes of city life. Now our daughter had been murdered in her own home in our town. Parents wondered: how safe is my child? It was hard for young people. They could not imagine someone their age being murdered in our community. Their anxiety level concerning their own safety reached new heights.

This is so hard—for our larger community.
Unfortunately, I was very slow in picking up on one need in our community. Often people in the community asked how we were doing. It was not unusual for that person to finally ask if an arrest had been made. On advice from the authorities I would reply that it had not yet been made. Six months later a friend asked that question one day. Either she asked it in a different way or I for the first time became sensitive, but suddenly I realized that people, especially women in the community, were afraid that the murderer was still roaming around, and they felt vulnerable. When I realized that, I quickly assured her that the suspect was no longer in the community. I could see the relief on her face. Then I realized how hard this was for the community, too. From that point on when anyone asked about the case, I realized that the question came not only from care and curiosity but also likely from fear, so I tried to relieve that fear as much as I could. He or she needed to be assured of some measure of safety.

This is so hard—physically.
The bomb had hit my body hard as well. My sleep

was medically induced and I was grateful for those hours of rest and amnesia of my loss. However the days revealed the weariness of grief. My normally high energy level was diminished. My body moved but felt like it was sagging all over. I continued to feel like a bomb had hit my body and was still dropping, a continual bomb coming down on me. It was the strangest physical feeling I have ever had.

A few weeks after Kym's death when I had gone back to work, a car eased into our driveway late one afternoon. A young teacher from the college where I taught, stepped out of the car with a hot chicken pie in her hands and said, "I brought you this because I know grieving is exhausting!" She was so right. Another lesson about grief I was learning.

As the busyness of the first week passed, some of the initial heaviness was relieved and then the heaviness of the realities weighed in. I would never see Kym's beautiful face again, or hear her say, "Mom, have you read Da Vinci Code? Why don't you buy it, and we can both read it?" There would be no more birthdays or Christmases or beach trips or ordinary days with her. She would never be older than 32. Her dreams would go unrealized because one person dared to take from her the most precious thing she had—her life!! I did not think I could bear this new reality. It hurt me all over my being. My young friend was so right. Grieving is exhausting. I needed to admit it and adjust my schedule accordingly.

This is so hard—spiritually.

Knowing that God cares was not hard. Not for one moment did I question God's love and care. Walking this journey without that divine presence was totally unthinkable. But knowing how to forgive and not be bitter was hard. It took a lot of walking and talking to God to deal with my attitude. I had to recognize and confess my weaknesses and flaws. My failures were not news to God! However, I discovered that I was not the Christian I thought I was. That recognition was sobering.

This is so hard—in a collection of ways.
This is so hard, but hard is not impossible. It is just hard. Kathleen O'Hara, a therapist whose son was murdered, says that surviving the violent death of a family member is ". . . a grief like no other. There is no warning, no time to say good-bye, no time to put things in order or tell the person whom you love the things you would want to. You will. . . instead be plunged into a world of terror and grief."[11] The suddenness and the violence collide to make the grief seem unbearable. She expressed my grief so well.

The bomb that never reaches bottom is loss. Grief is the work I have to do to heal the wounds of loss. The work of grief is so hard. I expect that when I draw my last breath it will still be so hard. Hard is not going away, but I am learning to live with hard.

Even as the bomb of loss kept dropping, I was already learning. I started making a list of things I was learning as a result of this experience. In a journal I

---

[11] O'Hara, 4

began keeping is this list:

When a person faces hard times she is bombarded with many different difficulties. Remember the many dimensions of hardship that she faces.

- When a person is in the midst of a crisis, remember to let him know I am thinking about him.
- Knowing that someone is willing to help makes hard a little easier.
- Be specific: I am going to the grocery store, what can I get for you? Let me take care of your yard. I can return your dishes.
- Be there. That someone cares enough to be with you matters.
- Listen and keep listening.
- Share a memory, a photo.
- Send a note or card or food several weeks later.
- Call months later to say I care.

God help me to remember what I have learned and act on it.

> *A child's sudden death adds more tasks to the complex work of grieving.. . .With the reality comes the painful knowledge that there have been no good-byes. No chance to sum up love or remember old pleasures. No chance to apologize for mistakes and insensitivities. No*

chance to hold her, tell her all that she has been to you[12]

Barbara Rosof in *The Worst Loss: How Families Heal from the Death of a Child.*

---

[12] Rosof, 193

Fragile Emotions

Blindside reminders is [a] term for the unexpected, unforeseeable event that seizes you unaware and floods you with memories. Sometimes the trigger is clear: a child who looks like yours, or a song on the radio. . .You feel exposed; you do not know how to protect yourself from these unbidden memories.

Barbara D. Rosof in *The Worse Loss: How Families Heal from the Death of a Child*[13]

Loss and emotions are partners. Sadness, helplessness, selfishness, guilt, anger—and the list goes on. Often those emotions reveal a characteristic better hidden. Very early on this journey I acted very

---

[13] Rosof, 83

badly. On the day of the visitation and memorial service our friends and family worked feverishly to arrange some mementos of Kym's life on tables in the foyer of our church. Bill and I went to the church early before the time for visitation so we could see what they had done. As we entered the foyer of the church some friends were already there and came over to speak to us. Immediately I barked that I came to see the tables and was not ready to see people yet. Thankfully Bill was more gracious than I and he visited with them. That incident has played most unhappily in my mind. Those folks probably had somewhere else to go and were kind enough to come by to see us before going on. It was quite clear from the beginning that I had to deal better with these fragile emotions.

Tears and I are not strangers! Tears flowed down my cheeks when I held our new baby or during a tender or sad moment in a movie. An intense argument with Bill usually results in tears for me. Tears have streamed down my face at weddings, sometimes even when I did not know the bride and groom! But tears did not come often and usually could be controlled. Now I am living with a flood that often comes when I least expect it—during a hymn, a compassionate remark from a friend, a sudden memory, reading a card or note, or getting a phone call. But most disconcerting is that sometimes tears flow for no identifiable reason; they just flow. Waves of sadness wash over me at times. I learned that I dare not be far away from tissues for I never know when I will need them.

Emotions swing so quickly. Sitting at the dining room table writing notes one day I felt a rush of love. I was sitting in front of an arrangement of beautiful flowers sent by a loving friend. I was writing thank you notes to people who expressed their sympathy in various ways. So many people cared for us, and I felt surrounded by that care and love. It was such a warm feeling. I was feeling loved and loving. Like a flash I suddenly thought they are expressing their love and compassion because some evil person took our daughter's life! In a split second I went from the warmth of love to the heat of anger! The mood swings were so unpredictable and so sharp. I often felt out of control. Some unseen force seemed to sway my feelings.

Faith is vital for me, and church is a source of strength and community. I needed church. I needed church as I had never needed church before. Its community, its hymns, and its messages were exactly what I needed to give me an anchor. But I also knew that if I went I would cry buckets of tears and be a distraction to any who sat near me. My solution was to slip into and out of church for several Sundays. After the service started I slipped into the balcony onto a bench next to the back wall. There I sat weeping as hymns were sung and listening with tears to the words of the sermon that seemed to be targeted just to me. Only the ushers knew I was there. As the closing hymn was sung, I slipped out. Being there helped immensely and I wasn't a distraction. Emotionally I was building up the ability to worship corporately as well as privately.

Like a bear in winter, I was hibernating. I did not want to bring a cloud of gloom to other people. I did not want to have one of those emotional surges in public, becoming a pitiful spectacle. Fear of being out of control was real for me. I was so emotionally fragile that I did not trust myself in public. I had never felt so emotionally vulnerable. It was a new and somewhat frightening experience. I was like a turtle in a shell fearful of sticking my head out. I needed to gain more confidence and stability before I ventured out.

Knowing that I could not hibernate forever, about three weeks after Kym's death I planned a quick trip to a local store. I walked in, fearing I would meet someone I knew and fall apart right there before everyone. Sure enough I did encounter four people. One person said a quick "hi" and rushed on to the next aisle as if nothing had changed for either of us. She had no idea she was going to run into me when she entered that store to shop and obviously was at a loss for words when she suddenly saw me, so she moved away quickly. Another spoke, asked how I was and rapidly moved on, clearly as uncomfortable as I was about this encounter. Upon turning into another aisle a friend looked up, saw me, spread her arms immediately and enveloped me in one of those treasured hugs, telling me how sorry she was. Impulsively she reacted with a warm embrace when she stumbled upon me. A cashier said that I did not know her, but she knew about our loss and wanted to give me a hug. She wrapped me in one of those wonderful warm hugs.

But this trip to the store had not gone as I expected! Walking to my car I had a profound revelation: my fear of seeing others was no greater than others' fear of seeing me! Anyone who chooses to go to a visitation, stands in a line, knowing she or he will come to the grieving family and say something to each person and/or hug them. That friend wants to say something or give a hug and comes to do so. But when a person rounds a display in a store and bumps into me, she is not prepared to see me or respond to me and is taken completely off guard. As I stayed home to avoid people, I now realized that some people would also want to avoid me. This was a two-way street.

Later I learned from Barbara Rosof that my experience is common. People are often uncomfortable around someone who is dealing with loss and in fact will avoid them if possible. Rosof advises the grieving to make the first move. I needed to work on that behavior!

Public display of emotions could not be completely avoided, and I knew that. And it was OK. For the first time in my life I was becoming comfortable with tears flowing wherever I was when they came—as long as I could refrain from sobbing. Sometimes kind people would say, "I don't want to make you cry" but the tears no longer bothered me although I realized they made others uncomfortable. I did not want to bawl and sob publicly, but tears were now a part of me. After an absence of three weeks from the classroom I returned to class. My first day back I talked about my loss and of course the tears streamed—a scene I could not have imagined three short weeks earlier. I am a new me. A sadder me.

A few days after Kym's death, our former pastor, said to me, "Carolyn, take care of yourself." At the time the last thing I was thinking of was taking care of myself. But the words stuck in my brain and as the days turned into weeks, I realized the wisdom of his words. It was quite clear that I could not take care of Kym. I really could not take away the grief from my family members. The only one I had control over was myself. He was right. I needed to work on taking care of myself.

Surges of grief came as I went through Kym's home deciding what to do with books, clothes, furniture and items dear to her, especially her collection of pigs. How she loved the things that gave expression to her life, the life now taken. More tears. Finding Christmas gifts already tucked away. More tears. So many reminders. So many unrealized plans. So much loss. Tears of loss. Permanent loss.

Almost a year and a half later when I thought I was doing pretty well with my emotions, a young Asian family came into the pew behind Bill and me as church began. I shook the hands of each of them and welcomed them. They were not the only Asians in our church and community and not the first I had seen or welcomed since Kym's death. I was glad to see the family. I shook the hands of the mother, father, young son, and a very shy young daughter about 8 or 9 years old. I had seen many young Asian girls since Kym died and usually had pleasant memories of Kym at that age. Occasionally I envied the family. For some totally unexplainable reason this day was different. As the church service got underway all I could think about was that girl who looked so much like Kym sitting behind me. The urge to turn around and envelope her in a warm and long hug overwhelmed me. I HAD to hug that precious child. It would be the closest thing to hugging Kym again. Tears were streaming down my cheeks, and I could not stop them. I knew I could not turn around and hug her during church, so I began to plan how I would approach her parents after church, explain the situation and ask their permission to allow me to hug their daughter. Recalling the child's shyness when I asked to shake her hand, I knew that a strange lady hugging her and probably crying would frighten the poor child. For fifteen or twenty minutes as tears flowed I argued with myself. Yes, I would try to hug her after church. No, I must not impose my grief on this innocent girl. Yes.

No. Yes. No. The tears kept coming. At one point I thought I would have to get up and leave the service lest I burst out sobbing. Finally I was able to convince myself that I must not meet my needs this way; I settled down. Almost a year and a half later I was still struggling with unexpected powerful emotions.

By this time I had read Barbara Rosof's book and searched for the passage about "blindside reminders" the "unexpected, unforeseeable event that seizes you unaware and floods you with memories. Sometimes the trigger is clear (another child, a song) and sometimes you cannot explain what crushes your chest and leaves you gasping. You feel exposed, you do not know how to protect yourself from these unbidden memories."[14] Reading that again, I thought "Did she ever nail that experience!"

Music still blindsides me frequently. Hymns that speak of God's care, of difficult times, of strength, of peace are especially emotional for me. Sometimes I can sing through tears and sometimes I have to become silent and just let the tears flow. Again I found assurance when I read Katheen O'Hara saying, "Music that wails will do some of your crying for you; music that is beautiful will give your hope and pleasure, in even your darkest moments."[15]

Fragile, unpredictable emotions. I am learning to live with them and to find a comfort level with them. My greater concern now is that they do not make others too uncomfortable. A few days after Kym's death a friend, who lost her son 32 years earlier, stood at our door speaking of that loss with tears rolling down her cheeks. Another friend, who lost a baby girl 48 years earlier, took me to lunch one day and when I mentioned her loss, tears welled up immediately in her eyes. From these two strong women I learned that the pain does not go away—ever. I must learn to live with the pain, the tears, and the emotions. And that is OK. A Chinese proverb says it well: You will often

---

[14] Ibid.

[15] O.Hara, 88

forget those you have laughed with, but you will never forget those you have cried with. Now I see those tears as a memorial to Kym, my love for her, and the tremendous void I will always feel with her absence.

Grief rearranges many emotion**s**. My books on grief gave me hope. Barbara Rosof helped me understand the importance of those emotions when she wrote of the paradox: "Only by allowing yourself to grieve. . .can you move toward a time and a place where the pain does not consume you. Only by allowing yourself to feel the most intense and shattering pain can you move toward a life in which pain is not the center."[16] She advised three principles: "allow yourself to feel what you feel, trust your own timetable for healing, and connect with other people."[17] Kathleen O'Hara wrapped me in a verbal hug when she gave this assurance: "Whenever you wonder if you have lost your mind, remind yourself: you have lost someone you love, not your mind."[18]

> *Every journey starts with a story: how it began, what happened, and where you are now. Your story is powerful, overwhelming; you will need to overcome it, manage it, and*

---

[16] Rosof, 50

[17] Rosof, 237

[18] O'Hara, 99

gain power over its raw emotions. And you will need to shape it into something you can carry so that its weight doesn't crush you; something you will bring with you across that ocean into a new world.[19]

Kathleen O'Hara in *A Grief Like No Other: Surviving the Violent Death of Someone You Love.*

---

[19] O,Hara, 2

Praying for Strength

The turbulence of your emotions may cause you to reexamine everything you thought you believed and will force you to do the hard work of deciding what, in fact, you do believe. When you emerge from this struggle, you will be that much stronger for it,. . .

Kathleen O'Hara in *A Grief Like No Other: Surviving the Violent Death of Someone You Love.*[20]

What do you pray for?" a friend inquired a couple of months after Kym's death. Without a pause I said, "Strength and peace." Strength was essential to make this journey totally foreign to me. I realized immediately that I needed boat loads of strength. In

---

[20] O.Hara, 38

fact, I didn't just need strength, I need strengths, many of them, a variety of strengths. God and I had a big job cut out for me!

My body needed strength.

This grief had attacked my whole system. Friends continued to bring food to nourish the body. Medication at bedtime allowed my body to gather strength for the following day. Walking in the neighborhood kept my body active. With the assistance of friends and physician I was still on my feet each day. Yet I felt like that bomb was still dropping on my whole system. I needed physical strength. Learning to pace myself helped. Day by day that strength came.

My emotions needed strength.

If my body was a wreck, my emotions were a disaster. Never had I been so vulnerable emotionally. I needed mega doses of strength to get back on my emotional feet. I was familiar with being physically exhausted and knew how to recover from that state. Emotional exhaustion was new to me. I needed a lot of help from God for this part of the journey. You name it, I needed it:

- Strength to go to the grocery store and know how to handle bumping into friends
- Strength to go to church without having an emotional meltdown
- Strength to go back to work, to focus on teaching, to be mentally clear enough to grade papers, to be engaged enough to participate in committees
- Strength to be the caregiver for my 92-year-old mother

- Strength to be a responsible family member— wife, mother, grandmother

God, give me strength!

My spirit needed strength.
Not for one minute did I believe that God wanted someone to take the life of our daughter. At these times in the human experience I believe God is grieved also. I believe God hurts when we hurt. And I remembered that God knows what it is like to have someone kill your child. My faith in God was unshakeable, even in this devastating moment of my life. What that faith meant in this time of crisis confronted me with new challenges: How will this experience shape my faith? How does my faith instruct my response to grief? As a Christian, how do I respond to the person who has murdered our daughter, who has violated our whole family? How does my faith instruct my emotions of anger, pain, uncertainty, loss, and agony? How do I sing the hymns of faith with new confidence? To this day tears roll down my cheeks when I sing Great is Thy Faithfulness and come to the words "Strength for today and bright hope for tomorrow" for that continues to be my prayer.

God, give me strength:
to put my feet on the floor and face another day,
to be honest with my emotions without becoming a burden to my friends,
to know as a person of faith how to handle this unfathomable crisis.
I need strength.

My need for friends.

Again Barbara Rosof gave me focus. Much of my grieving may be silent, inward, solitary, she suggested. I would need to deal with many aspects of my loss alone. But my strength to keep going would also come from other people—who cared for me, understood my pain, believed I could rebuild. I could not do this alone.

How would I ever walk this journey without strength that came from friends? The calls, cards, emails, caring questions of concern that continued to come, let me know that others were walking this journey with me. Knowing that I was not alone in my grief was another source of strength.

And yet I had to work on gaining strength myself, little by little. When I go for a walk around our neighborhood, the worst part of that walk is the end when I climb the steep hill up to our house. I have learned that the best method of walking up that hill is to look down at the pavement and take one step at a time. If I look up it seems too hard, and my body starts bending in response. When I focus on one step at a time I stay erect and focus on just this step. That idea has also guided me with living day to day with grief. I ask God for strength just for this day. One day at a time.

> *Strength for today and bright hope for tomorrow.*
>
> From the hymn *Great is Thy Faithfulness*, words by Thomas O. Chisholm

Praying for Peace

. . . everything can be taken from a man but one thing: the last of the human freedoms--- to choose one's attitude in any given set of circumstances, to choose one's own way.
— Viktor Frankl

Kathleen O'Hara in *A Grief Like No Other: Surviving the Violent Death of Someone You Love.*[21]

What do you pray for?" my friend asked. "Strength and peace," I replied. "Which do you want most?" Without batting an eye I said, "Peace." As much as I wanted and needed strength, more than anything else I craved peace. Four words, "Carolyn, Kym is dead," shocked me out of a normal life into sheer turmoil: Police officers, district attorneys, and

---

[21] O'Hara, 48

state investigators were now a part of our lives. News reporters from television and print media wanted information. How do we get through the military bureaucracy to get in touch with Kym's dear friend? I completely forgot about responsibilities at work I was so out of touch. Friends came to our rescue, handling the media for us, taking care of my work responsibilities before I even thought about them. Suddenly in one brief moment my life was in turmoil. The initial shock soon gave way to a swirl of changes and uncertainties.

In the midst of the turmoil I was wrestling with disturbing and in some cases horrible facts:

- Someone had taken the life of our daughter.
- Her last moments on earth were unbelievably frightening and I had been unable to prevent it.
- Kym's brothers had found her body and were reeling from that discovery.
- "I was haunted by the question of why someone would want to kill her.
- I had very strong emotions regarding this unknown person.
- That person who took her life had changed my life forever.
- I had a range of strong emotions unlike I had ever had.

I needed peace, abundant peace. Being captive of the angry feelings associated with these facts could easily lead me into a life time of bitterness. One thing I knew for sure: I did not want to live the rest of my life in bitterness, a person who lived in anger. I had to have peace in order to avoid becoming an emotional cripple. That person took one life, I refused to let him (I assumed a male) take my life, which is-- my emotional health, also.

My attitude

I could not change this tragedy. The only thing I could control was my attitude toward it. Eventually I read of Kathleen O'Hara's grief over the murder of her son. She reminded me that it is "difficult to change my perception and expectations of the world I lived in. But if I was to have any peace at all, I would have to find the courage to change what I could— myself."[22]   She added that survival depends on making changes and the only thing you have power to change is yourself. So that is where you must start. OK, so I had to start working on the peace initiative.

With God's help I would live in peace; but it was going to take a lot of work on God's part and on mine. Right away I realized that God would not give me peace unless I was willing to work on it myself. So I walked and talked: talked to God about wanting peace, talked to God about what peace could bring to my life, talked to God about how hard it was to deal with my anger, talked to God about my stabbing pain, about the depth of loss I felt, and begged for peace. I did not want to live the rest of my life as a bitter old

---

[22] O'Hara, 130

woman. Kym was a person who lived life to the fullest. Ending my life as a bitter person would not respect her spirit, only a meaningful life would.

My work

Quickly I realized that I had to work with God on this peace-seeking task. Peace would not come if I prayed for it and then refused to make any effort on my part. God and I were partners in this effort, and I had to be a willing receptacle for this gift, this grace of peace. My neighbor left a post-it note with Psalm 34:18 written on it: "The Lord is near to the broken-hearted." I stuck it on the fridge to remind me of the source of genuine peace.

A quotation from an unknown source was so helpful that I jotted it down and put it on my desk so that I saw it every day: "What might have been does not exist, so don't go there." I would not find peace if I focused entirely on what might have been, and that was so very tempting. It was so easy to painfully dream of what Kym's life would have been had she lived more than 32 years. My grief and the loss I felt centered on all that was loss for her and for us. But those "might have beens" did not exist and would not. Soon I learned that I would "go there" often and grieve the "might have beens" and that was OK; it was part of remembering Kym. But I also learned that to have peace I could not stay there. Peace would come when I came to terms with what has been and began moving forward toward what could be. This was the work I had to do for myself.

My reading

Books on grief written by counseling professionals and by persons who had traveled the paths of grief were helpful to me. Learning how others came to terms with their sad realities gave me hope. Kathleen O'Hara pointed me toward three helpful principles: acceptance, forgiveness, and gratitude. "Acceptance asks us to recognize what we can change and what we cannot—and ask for the wisdom to understand the difference. Forgiveness helps us to work on our feelings of anger, hatred, and revenge, which inevitably harmed us more than the person to whom they are directed. Gratitude helps us recognize what has been given, taken away, and remains after the storms have passed."[23] She added, "when you stop fighting the ocean, then you can move out of the deep."[24]

She challenged me to change the things I can: myself, the way I think, how I look at and respond to events over which I have no control. So when I asked, why Kym? I had to also ask, why not? Is my child more precious than anyone else's?

Scripture and reading from religious classics brought assurance of God's presence on this journey to peace. Lines from a familiar hymn became my prayer:

---

[23] O'Hara, 121

[24] O'Hara, 129

Drop thy still dews of quietness
Till all my strivings cease
Take from my soul the strain and stress
And let my ordered life confess
The beauty of thy peace.[25]

Many mornings I drove to work singing those words. They tended to settle me.

My gratitude
In the middle of this peace work I was doing, my pastor called asking me to preach for him in a couple of months when he would be away. I thought about it for a while, called him back and said I would, thinking that I could use a sermon I had prepared for another occasion. Soon I realized that this was an opportunity for me to give voice to my need to look forward. This was an opportunity for me to remind myself and the audience of the many ways we had been blessed. Focusing on that message pushed me to assess the abundance of blessings in my life—to see this tragedy as a very ugly part of a life that has been blessed. That perspective countered my urges toward bitterness.

Placing my current heartbreak into the larger context of my life, I became more aware of how full and blessed my life had been. And from the first day of this crisis I realized that even in the midst of tragedy

---

[25] Lines adapted from the hymn Dear Lord and Father of Mankind, words by John G. Whittier.

we had some things for which to be grateful. Within a few weeks I began to make a list of things for which I was thankful. We had a body. Some families have a missing person who is found much later in a wooded area or isn't found at all. We knew where her body was from the first moment. Her sister and brothers all lived out of town but were all in town that day because of their grandmother's funeral. So our family was immediately together with each other and for each other. We were surrounded by friends, enveloped by their love and support. And within a few days there was a solid suspect so the mystery and uncertainty of not knowing who was responsible was relieved.

I could wallow in pity and at times I was up to my neck in a pit of pity. But that pit is an ugly place to dwell. Going back to read my thankful list helped. I could try to focus on where I found gratitude. Would I wallow in pity over the years Kym would not live or would I bathe in the memories of the 32 years she did live? That was MY choice. One of those choices would keep me in turmoil. The other could lead me to peace. If God gave me peace I had to be ready to receive it. Some days I did not want it. Increasingly I yearned for it and the freedom from anger that it brought.

Peace is work and peace is gift.
Peace is an incredible gift. I cherish every level of peace that I have. But peace is work, ongoing work. In fact peace is actually a journey, a continuing process, not a destination. Some days I have more of it than others.

Our August Saturday morning was terribly and horribly broken. But the song "Morning Has Broken" sung at the memorial service for Kym pointed us to hope. "Praise every morning God's re-creation of the new day."

Sorting the Guilt

Be kind to yourself. Perfection is not necessary; there is no arriving, only going. There is no need to judge where you are in your journey. It is enough that you are traveling.

Brook Noel and Pamela D. Blair in *I Wasn't Ready to Say Goodbye: Surviving, Coping and Healing after the Sudden Death of a Loved One*[26]

Without warning my sandwich was crumbling. What remained was very raw. I was a caretaker for my 92-year-old mother, residing in a local retirement home. Our youngest daughter who was single had returned to our hometown. I was glad to have them both in town. This was a typical scenario

---

[26] Noel and Blair, 183

of what is called the "sandwich generation." I was the middle of these two generations. Mother was the oldest member of my family; Kym, the youngest. I was the linking generation. Ten weeks after Kym died, my mother waved her fingers "goodbye" and breathed her last breath. In less than three months both of them were dead. I would have never dreamed of that scenario. My sandwich crumbled so quickly, unexpectedly, and tragically that I was left with very raw emotions.

My heart was broken

My heart was broken, and my brain was limping. And the two of them were at war. My heart was loaded with guilt related to both deaths. Even my limping brain knew the folly of that guilt but knowing did not erase the guilt. For days and weeks after Kym died I felt so guilty that I was not with her during those horrible moments when her killer was taking all that was precious from her. "If I had only been there," I told myself repeatedly this would not have happened. "If I, or anyone, had been with her there would have been two of us against the killer. We would have prevented her death, and she would still be alive." That is what my heart said over and over.

My brain was limping

My limping brain reminded me that Kym prided herself on living alone and taking care of herself. Why in the world would I have ever been standing by on that evening? Of course I would not have gone home with her that evening to protect her. Neither she nor I knew she was in danger. Why would I have been there, my brain said. But I should have, my heart said, then she would be alive. Guilt that I had not prevented her death

61

haunted me. Her mother ought to protect her from such a fate, my heart said. Mothers can't always do that, my brain said. And so the argument between heart and head continued regularly for months and still surfaces from time to time.

Mother was declining

In the meantime, Mother's gradual decline of the last three years now began to become more rapid and noticeable. It became clear on a daily basis that the woman who had bounced back repeatedly the last three years was likely not going to bounce back after losing her good friend and her granddaughter in the same week. The woman who had loved to read, to keep up with the news, and to talk, now spent more time in silence looking out the window of her apartment. She needed me more and at a new level than at any time previously. And I was there on a daily basis, sometimes more than once, but as an emotional cripple myself, I did not have the ability to be there in a way I would have a month earlier. I could talk to her about Kym and about Bill's Mother, but I could not prod her to talk about her grief as I should have. I was too fragile myself to go there with her. And so she walked that journey more alone than I could have ever wished. That guilt still troubles me.

My broken heart said I should have been a better daughter to her during that time. My limping brain told me that I was doing the best I could, that Mother was not always prone to talk about her deep feelings and may not have wanted me to prod her to do so. My heart said, but how do I know, for I never tried.

In those ten weeks, I took her to the Emergency Room

twice and tended to her medical needs. As a person who has always been afraid to be alone at night, she felt very safe in the third-floor apartment of her retirement home. But after Kym's death she began to barricade her bedroom door at night. When I realized that Kym's violent death had awakened her old fears, we engaged sitters for her around the clock. Her funds were running low, but so was her life. We needed her to feel safe and to do so she needed to know someone was with her all night as well as day and those were provided. When I became aware that she might qualify for hospice, she was enrolled. What a gift that service was to her and to me. Now she had twenty-four-hour sitters, an excellent and attentive retirement home staff, and hospice, but I still felt guilty.

I believed that she still needed me emotionally at a level I could not produce. My brain said I did my best. My heart said she needed more. Her last three days she was bedfast. As I left each night I wondered if she would live through the night and thought I should stay with her. But I knew my physical and emotional state was not up to staying with her around the clock especially since I had no idea how long she would last in that weakened state. And so she died at 4:30 AM and I was not there! My heart said I should have been there. My head said I did not know she was going to die then.

What do I do with guilt?
Sorting my guilt is an ongoing task that still bubbles up. The hospice material that came regularly after mother's death was most helpful in assisting me in processing both her death and Kym's. Some of that information

dealt with guilt and was helpful, but I still struggle with that war of the emotional and intellectual understanding of how I responded to both deaths. My "oughts" and my "coulds" are in sharp conflict.

Two voices leaped from the pages I was reading. Brook Noel and Pamela Blair in *I Wasn't Ready to Say Goodbye* seemed to be speaking to me directly. "Realize this guilt is a way of trying to gain control over the uncontrollable and then work to let it go...You cannot change what has happened and odds are you couldn't have changed it beforehand."[27] I read that passage again and again. Of course I cannot change what happened. And could I realistically have prevented it? No, so my guilt is about trying to control what was uncontrollable. My challenge is to face that reality. Dealing with guilt is a struggle *that continues.*

> *When you become tired of beating yourself up for not controlling everything, stop, take a breath, and let go. It's over, nothing will change that.*[28]

> Kathleen O'Hara in *A Grief Like No Other; Surviving the Violent Death of Someone You Love*

---

[27] Noel and Blair, 32

[28] O'Hara, 101

What is Closure?

Closure does not mean forgetting or dismissing. . .it means recognizing that you have done one piece of painful work and now can turn to the next task. Of all the ways in which a parent loses a child, murder may be the most difficult to bring some closure to.

Barbara D. Rosof in *The Worst Loss: How Families Heal from the Death of a child* [29]

After about a year people began to say very compassionately, "I hope you soon get closure." I heard a lot of care and concern in those words. But after a while I began to ask myself, what is closure? The more I pondered the question, the more uncertain I was about what it was. The dictionary did not help. So I began to wrestle with this concept of

---

[29] Rosof, 216

closure, for I had said it to others myself. What did I mean? What do they mean?

Is it forgetting?

That is not possible. To forget what happened is to dishonor Kym. To forget her is to dismiss the spunky contribution she made to the lives of our family members. To forget the tragedy of her death is to deny a deep wound. Of course our friends did not want us to forget her. That is not what they meant by closure.

Is it an absence of pain?

Is closure getting past the pain? I don't think so. My experience so far and the experiences shared with us by others who have traveled this journey affirm that the pain does not go away as long as we live. To escape the pain is not realistic. To escape the pain would say our loss was only temporary, which it is not. Perhaps my friends really would like for our family to be rid of the pain, but I know they realize that really will not happen. So I do not think they are honestly wishing our pain will go away.

Is it putting the past behind you?

The dictionary meanings of closure focus on shutting off. No doubt in their compassion our friends would have wished we could shut off the painful past, close the door on those events, remove them from our thinking. That is a very loving wish for a hurting friend. But all of us, my friends and I, know that will not happen either.

Is it getting on with your life?

I suppose this is a part of what we mean when we want closure for another person. But as I pondered this definition of closure, I realized that we had done that from the beginning. Within two hours of discovering Kym's body our family was at the funeral for Bill's mother. And the next morning and all the mornings after we got up and started another day. We HAD to get on with our lives. To be honest, we did not have any other choice. And gradually our lives resumed their routines. If closure means getting on with life, we were already in the process of doing that.

Is it getting answers to your myriad of questions?

The more I thought about it, the more I thought that perhaps this is what closure meant. Our friends did not want us to lose a daughter and not have answers regarding her death. We wanted those answers also. Already we had some answers that the public did not have, and those answers did help us cope in some ways. Of course, our desire for answers would solve some of the mystery and perhaps that is a form of closure.

Is it getting justice?

Perhaps in this case, closure meant getting justice. Did the wish for closure mean that our friends wanted justice to be served, giving us some solace? Maybe that was what closure meant. We did want justice. The person who took Kym's life must be punished, must pay a price for such an evil act. But justice would not compensate for our loss.

Is it possible?

I began to wonder if closure is even possible. When your child's life is taken, the lives of every member of your family are permanently altered. There is a big hole in the family, a vacuum that will never be filled. How can there ever be closure, or a shutting off, of such a loss?

By now Kathleen O'Hara was like a cherished friend. Her words were like a treasured find when I saw . . ."you are still grieving and, as much as you and everyone else would like to achieve closure, you cannot. This word closure is one which I and many other survivors detest. There is no 'closure.' This grief, like no other, will be a life-long journey. People will insist we have closure, because they think it will be better for us and for them."[30] Yes! Now I know that for me, closure is not possible. And that's OK. I can live with no closure. In my way of thinking, no closure means that Kym is still very much a part of our family, if only in memory now.

Once when a friend I knew well said she would be glad when we had closure, I asked her what that meant. Her eyes froze and her tongue became mute. When she got her voice, she replied that she did not know, that she had never thought about what she really meant.

When I hear someone say she wants closure for our family, I don't try to figure out what she means, I

---

[30] O'Hara, 120

assume that she is wishing the best for us. I am glad to have friends who continue to care, who realize that it is a long and difficult journey. I believe they want our journey of pain to become a journey of peace. And so do I.

> *Acceptance is a process that we experience, not a final stage with an end point.*
>
> Elisabeth Kubler-Ross and David Kressler in *On Grief and Grieving*[31]

> *Acceptance is a process that we experience, not a final stage with an end point.*
>
> Elisabeth Kubler-Ross and David Kressler in *On Grief and Grieving*[1]

---

[31] Kubler-Ross, and Kessler, 27

I'm OK; I'm Fine

For the job you have—grieving—you have no blueprint.

Barbara Rosof in *The Worst Loss: How Families Heal from the Death of a Child*[32]

Hi, how are you?" is such a common greeting we give little thought to it. After Kym's death I heard those words differently. How was I? I was a physical and emotional wreck! But when someone asked they did not want to hear me say that of course. To say "I'm fine" was a bold-faced lie and most people who asked would know it was. So my dilemma was how to answer that question as honestly as I could without being a walking rain cloud: I mustn't say that I was a wreck. I mustn't lie and say that I was fine. Why rain on someone else's day by saying that I was hurting so badly I wanted to cry? Sometimes I could have said that I was the worst I had ever been.

---

[32] Rosof, 257

The list of options often changed from day to day. The question "how are you?" that I ask of others, and they ask of me is a perfunctory one. Most of us really do not want to know any details. We expect a perfunctory answer. I realized that. So how was I going to handle that very perfunctory question in a way that I found comfortable? I finally was most comfortable saying, "I'm OK." That was a good perfunctory answer I thought and considering the situation it was honest, for I was OK.

For many months that was my regular answer, "I'm OK." As the year progressed I was increasingly thankful to be OK. Then one day I heard myself respond, "I'm fine." That was a crucial moment, another milestone toward some new kind of normalcy. "I'm fine." There was a lot of progress behind that statement. But it was a new kind of fine.

In our community lived an active lady with a career in business, a husband, and two daughters. A very intelligent and capable woman, she struggled in her senior years with a heart condition and a stroke. After each episode she fought back and soon returned to church, moving more slowly but very surely. I was so glad to see her back one of those times and of course asked, "How are you?" She replied, "I'm fine; but fine is not what it used to be." She was so right.

The definition of "fine" changes. I am fine now, but fine now is not what it used to be. And some days I am back to OK again, but that's OK too. Every day is not a "fine" day, but every day is a gift and that I am OK on that day is a double gift.

Being OK is fine.

> *You never forget what you lost. You learn to value what you have.*
>
> Barbara Rosof in *The Worst Loss: How Families Heal from the Death of a Child*[33]

---

[33] Rosof, 269

Many Kinds of Grief

*During an average lifetime there are many
pains, many grieves to be borne. We don't
'get over' them; we learn to live with them, to
go on growing and deepening, and
understanding.*

Madeleine L'Engle, *Sold Into Egypt*[34]

Two years before Kym died I thought I knew grief,
and I did at one level. The phone rang on a
Sunday afternoon the second week in January 2002,
and we learned that our oldest daughter and her
husband were starting the process of getting a
divorce. The next eighteen months I discovered a
new kind of grief, and it had many layers: I was
certain the marriage could be repaired and not ended;
I was wrong. Soon I realized that the pain that our
daughter was experiencing was one I could not heal:
the breaking up of the home of our two

---

[34] As quoted in Noel and Blair, 47

grandchildren, the rawness of the issues, the lawyers, the custody arrangements, the physical tasks of separating, and the emotional tasks of separating. There was so much pain in our daughter's life that I could do little about it. Then the grief and pain arose at another level for I realized that our extended family was forever changed. Those times at the beach, at Christmas or other holidays would not include this family of four, but only three of them—and maybe not all three because the children would now be rotating between parents at those times. Eventually I realized that my dream of family times crowded with all the children, all the grandchildren, a big happy family, was not going to be. I had to bury my dream. I was surprised by how hard it was to bury that dream.

Five months after our daughter and her husband established separate homes, in the spring of 2003 our oldest son and his wife in another state separated. I thought I could not handle any more. I was still in the recovery room from the last surgery our family had experienced! Once more I was sure this marriage could be repaired. Again I was mistaken. (Our children seem to think they know more about their marriage relationships than I do!) Two more grandchildren were going to live between two homes. Ten months later in the spring of 2004 they finalized their divorce. It seemed like life could not get worse, or at least that is the way it felt emotionally. If someone had asked me if it could get worse, I could have acknowledged that everyone was still alive and healthy and that was a lot to be grateful for. However, at the time all I could focus on was how two of our children in the span of a little over a year had gotten divorces. Once upon a time I had said that with four children in our family, the odds of one of them getting a divorce were good. Saying it and living it are two entirely different things. Clearly I had never really come to terms with that reality, and I surely had not even conceived of two divorces within two years. Life was becoming too painful!

All of this was pressing in on me one day as I drove home from work crying and telling God in no uncertain terms that I did not deserve this kind of hurt.--a remark I quickly repented of when I realized how many good things had come my way that I did not deserve. I backtracked on my edict to God about what I deserved very fast!

But that experience did reveal how very deep the hurt was for the family members beyond the immediate family getting the divorce. While a divorce is a major trauma and adjustment to the parents and children, it is also an adjustment of lesser but still traumatic proportions to the extended family. Divorce is the death of a marriage and is also a journey of grief. So much of our lives was permanently rearranged and that journey of grief is one of pain and peace as well.

Then I discovered there was an even deeper grief in August of 2004 when Kym's body was discovered. Almost one year later I wrote in my journal: "If I were writing a book now about this experience I would give it the title Living with Sadness in 3-D. The **three** crises of our children—two divorces and a death; the **three** deaths of Kym and our mothers in ten weeks; and all of this within **three** years."

Yes, I was learning there are many kinds of grief. There was also the grief for losing the old me. I am a different "me." For I have been forever changed.

> *This sense of entitlement to a pain-free existence and the alienation from one another and from the truth about life it breeds can be more isolating than suffering itself.*
>
> Kathleen Brehony in *After the Darkest Hour: How Suffering Begins the Journey to Wisdom*[35]

---

[35] Brehony, 34-35

Moving On

Your story is. . . woven into the new life you build; it is the warp and weave of everything you do, inseparable from the person you have become.

Kathleen O'Hara in *A Grief Like No Other: Surviving the Violent Death of Someone You Love,*[36]

Friends want us to move on. We want to move on. But how do we move on when we hurt so badly? When a stranger has stolen the life of our daughter? When we have such a hole in our hearts? When our lives have been permanently altered? How do we find peace when there is so much pain?

It was very comforting to me to see Kathleen O'Hara saying that your love for the person and your grief

---

[36] O'Hara, 197

keeps you "rooted in your loved one's horrible last moments. . . The thought of moving on is not only repugnant to you but seems impossible." Moving on is "like saying you are healed which you are not."[37] Yes, Ms. O'Hara you are so right! Emotionally it is repugnant, and it does seem totally impossible. But she did not leave me there. Soon I read these words: ". . . you will take your loved one along within you no matter where you go or what you do. You are *both* moving forward."[38]

But just what is moving on? Moving on is so many things. Moving on . . .

Is unavoidable
Each day forces it, there is no way out. From the first morning I put my feet on the floor, facing a day I never dreamed I would face, I was moving on. I had started another day. Moving on starts immediately. Every day, week, month, and year is pushing me to move on. Some folks may move faster. Some may get stuck at one place and not go beyond it. But moving on is unavoidable, even if it is only one step such as getting through the rituals. How far and how quickly I go forward depends on me as an individual as well as many other factors. But I will move on. There is no other choice. Whether I move on in positive ways or negative ones depends on the choices I make.

---

[37] O'Hara, 194

[38] O'Hara, 195

Is difficult

Moving on is difficult because I often feel stuck. Life is permanently changed. I don't know what all that means yet, but I do know it is painful. I have never been this way. I have no map. I am emotionally uncertain. To begin with I will do only the emotional work that is minimal. To be honest what I really want to do is to curl up, suck my thumb, and grab my blanket. Moving on is difficult. Oh, if there were a way to escape this journey!

Is expected

Moving on is expected by others and by me. When we speak of moving on, I think we are saying we want life to be back to "normal." Friends want normal. I want normal--whatever normal is going to be now. Both are unrealistic expectations. Friends want us to move on much faster than we can; it gives them a comfort level. I want to move on, lest I wear them out with my woes. Everyone wants to put the pain, the trauma behind them. Life is better for all when it is peaceful and not painful.

Is backward

I want to move on, and I like those days when I feel I have, although those are scary feelings. I do make some progress. Then one of those waves hits, knocking me back off my feet for a while. Moving on is not a series of steady steps forward. It is a few steps forward and then some backward. The whole journey does progress but moving on goes backward at times before it goes on. Before I go into drive I have to get out of reverse.

Is peace and pain

The peace I long for begins to come more often and that feels like moving on and it is. However, pain rears its head at unexpected moments interrupting the peace. Dealing with the pain is often a way of moving on. In fact, a false peace can impede moving on. Moving on is not a steady climb up a mountain of grief to the peak of peace but walking through the valleys of pain that keep intruding on the climb. Moving on does not mean that pain is erased and replaced by tranquility and serenity. Moving on means learning how to live with and learn from the pain.

Is helped by friends who remember
In *The Worse Loss* Barbara Rosof says that "to heal and rebuild we need the help of other people. . . [to] listen to your story, appreciate the depth of your pain, assure you that you are not going crazy. . . who understand the magnitude of your loss and the size of the job you face, who respect your journey, no matter how halting or detoured."[39]   While most of our friends quickly returned to their routines as they should, it was most helpful to our family that a few friends continued to remember how difficult moving on is. A card or email from one friend seemed to come on just the right day in the months and years that followed. Or a lunch conversation with another friend helped me to move on with less of a limp. A phone call from a friend asking how I was doing seemed well-timed to let me go backward a bit before I moved on.

---

[39] Rosof, 140

At times I was hesitant to talk about my grief again to someone. I did not want people to dread seeing me coming, thinking all I could talk about was grief. So it was helpful for me to read more words of Barbara Rosof: "To bear the intense pain and disorientation of acute grief you need people to help you with the mechanics of your life, buffer you from the world, listen to your story, appreciate the depth of your pain, assure you that you are not going crazy."[40]

About a year after Kym's death I wrote this in a journal I was keeping about this journey:

"This would be such a lonelier and much more difficult journey without caring friends. Knowing that another person cares does not eliminate the grief, but it makes it somewhat easier to bear."

Is very complicated
About the same time I noted, "There are times that I feel Kym's spirit or perhaps presence. That does not convey what I feel very well but are the closest words I can find to express it. It is a good feeling usually, although when I left her grave yesterday, it was like she was saying, 'Mom, don't leave me.'"

Moving on is complicated and it starts on day one. It is an uncertain path, full of detours.

I found this prayer in *I Wasn't Ready to Say Goodbye*. It gave me hope about moving on.

---

[40] Ibid.

Prayer of Faith

We trust that beyond absence
there is a presence.

That beyond the pain
there can be healing.

That beyond the brokenness
there can be wholeness.

That beyond the anger
there may be peace.

That beyond the hurting
there may be forgiveness.

That beyond the silence
there may be the Word.

That beyond the Word
there may be understanding.

That through understanding
there is love.

Author unknown[41]

I am not sure what moving on is for me. But there is a passage of scripture that is my basis for understanding life: Ecclesiastes 3: 1-8. This text reminds me of the rhythms of life, seasons that come

---

[41] Noel and Blair, 39

and go. Life is a series of ups and downs that are realistically expressed in this passage:

> *For everything there is a season,*
> *and a time for every matter under heaven:*
> *a time to be born, and a time to die;*
> *a time to plant, and a time to pluck up*
> *what is planted;*
> *a time to kill, and a time to heal;*
> *a time to break down, and a time to build*
> *up;*
> *a time to weep, and a time to laugh;*
> *a time to mourn, and a time to dance;*
> *a time to throw away stones, and a time to*
> *gather stones together;*
> *a time to embrace, and a time to refrain from*
> *embracing;*
> *a time to seek, and a time to lose;*
> *a time to keep, and a time to throw away;*
> *a time to tear, and a time to sew;*
> *a time to keep silence, and a time to speak;*
> *a time to love, and a time to hate;*
> *a time for war, and a time for peace.* [42]

No, I do not believe that this passage sanctions the murder of our daughter when it speaks of death and killing. I do believe that the writer recognizes that life is complex. Life isn't simple and cannot be explained simply.

---

[42] The Holy Bible: New Revised Standard Version (New York: HarperCollins Publishers, 2008)

Our family has been in one of the weeping, mourning seasons of life. However, we will laugh and dance again.

> Blessed be the Lord, for he has heard the sound of my pleadings. The Lord is my strength and my shield; to him my heart trusts; so I am helped, and my heart exults, and with my song I give thanks to him.
> Psalm 28:6-7[43]

---

[43] Ibid.

Don't Tell Unless Asked

Telling the story helps to dissipate the pain. Telling your story often and in detail is primal to the grieving process.

Elisabeth Kubler-Ross and David Kessler in *On Grief and Grieving,* [44]

People vary in their interest in your journey of loss. Some people do not want to hear any more, so don't tell. Other people are willing to hear more and ask. Those are the folks you tell. People have various reasons for not wanting to hear more, and I don't know what those reasons are, but I am sure they are valid. Who knows what is going on in their lives that I do not know, so I just accept that they have reasons, good reasons, for not asking. One of those reasons may be that they simply do not want to hear any more about our troubles. All of us have our limits on bearing other peoples' burdens.

---

[44] Kubler-Ross and Kessler, 63

Kindly the lady behind the counter said, "I have not asked you about how you are doing since Kym's death, because I did not want to bring it up and hurt you." I replied, "I hurt when you don't bring it up and I hurt when you do bring it up because I hurt all the time. It is OK to ask."

Other people have reasons for asking and I do not know what they are, but they ask, and I tell. It helps so much to know that they still remember and care. The telling is helpful to me. A parent told Barbara Rosof, "When we talk about Ray, I feel like I'm keeping him alive. Not literally. . . But talking about him helps my memories of him stay stronger, especially the good ones. It's like watering a garden."[45] I love it when folks ask about Kym, her death or her life. They remember her! She still lives in their memory. She is not forgotten. Her living has not been in vain.

Six years after Kym's death Bill walked into an office for a meeting. Sitting behind the desk was one of Kym's friends. When she saw him she said, "At our 20th high school reunion recently we talked about Kym and how much we missed her." Her classmates remembered her. What a gift for Bill that day! Memories are all that remain and they are more precious than diamonds or gold.

---

[45] Rosof, 11

This "don't tell unless asked" reality is the reason support groups are formed so that those who need to talk will have willing and empathic ears to hear. Other friends are then spared. I shall forever be grateful to special friends who keep on asking.

> . . .*what we offer in caring and in assurance that the other is not alone is the strongest, truest help we can give each other.*
>
> Barbara Rosof in *The Worst Loss: How Families Heal from the Death of a Child*[46]

> . . .*what we offer in caring and in assurance that the other is not alone is the strongest, truest help we can give each other.*
>
> Barbara Rosof in *The Worst Loss: How Families Heal from the Death of a Child*[2]

---

[46] Rosof, xi

Remembering Anniversaries

The [anniversary] day passed, and I was grateful I'd gotten through one whole year. If I had done that, surely I could do it again.

Kathleen O'Hara in *A Grief Like No Other: Surviving the Violent Death of Someone You Love*[47]

As the anniversary of Kym's death drew nearer, I had a train load of feelings. It appeared I had made the trip around the calendar, through holidays, her birthday, Mother's Day, etc. One more day lay ahead, the anniversary of her death. And which day was it? The day her brothers found her (the official date) or the day we think she actually died? There is some irony in the fact that we do not know the exact date of her death for we do not know the exact date of her birth. Her caring parents left her as a newborn

---

[47] O'Hara, 117

in a safe place where she would be found and cared for. She was taken immediately to a hospital where the nurses guessed at her birth date. Now we guess at the date of her death. From birth to death Kym was enveloped in mystery. Whatever date we choose to mark her death, it is a defining date in the life of our family. The anniversary of her death marks the day that divides our family life into what was and what is. Barbara Rosof summarizes the first anniversary experience poignantly when she concludes that by end of that first year "you have learned more than you ever cared to know about pain and your own capacity to bear it."[48] Yes, we have. I had no idea a year ago what pain and loss I could bear. And I sure wish I had never found out! However, there was certainly some personal growth and a budding peace in the process.

It meant so much when various people remembered that first anniversary of Kym's death. It helped to know people remembered her. It helped to know people still cared about our loss. It helped when some anonymous person put flowers in the church on the anniversary of her birth and death. She was remembered.

On that day I observed in my journal "I have dreaded this day but am learning that sometimes my 'dreads' are worse than the days. Or perhaps my 'dreads' prepare me for those days." For an entire year I had dreaded what lay ahead, whatever holiday or family

---

[48] Rosof, 252

day or Kym day was coming up on the calendar. In 31 years I had not experienced that day or time without her. I had expected to share those days with her till I died, and now she was gone forever. What would that be like? I did not know what Christmas, or her birthday would be like, or our family's trip to the beach. I dreaded those times. I dreaded her keen absence, not seeing her pretty smile, hearing her sassy remarks, or feeling her warm hug. How could I go through those days feeling the vacuum of her death? Dread. That was the word. In reflection, dread seemed to have prepared me for those days. While those days were not as bad as I feared, they were bad enough. Expecting the worst likely made the reality easier. One trip around the calendar year gave me the knowledge of what those days would be like. As Suzanne said these days were the last of our firsts. One more way to move on.

Remembering Kym on the anniversary of her death meant going to the cemetery for me. Her name on the marker, the items left there by her friends, and the flowers I left there was the closest I could be to her that day. It is not easy for any mother to stand at the grave of her child. On my way home loss was overcome by anger. I had a long, tearful "talk" with the suspect, telling him how much he took from Kym, from us, how much he hurt us, how much he has surely hurt his Mother and his own little boy--and all because of his own selfishness and evilness. He caused so much long-term hurt due to one selfish, evil, impulsive act. More pain than peace on that day.

Each family member experienced the day uniquely. Alan, who first discovered her body, was busy out of town that day for which he was grateful. Art who had been there when the body was found, had a moving experience at a cemetery in Denver where a circling bird led him to the grave of a young woman named Blevins where he left roses. Suzanne had a good visit with her Stephen minister. Bill was dealing with the double anniversaries of the death of his mother and his daughter.

During the weekend of that anniversary we were showered with cards, calls, and emails from Kym's friends and ours. Two of her college friends came from out of town to visit and tell "Kym stories." Unfortunately some of our friends had also traveled the road of losing a child and were especially thoughtful. It was so meaningful and helpful to be reminded that others remembered the day and our grief.

At the end of the day I wrote, "One year ago today our world fell apart and we have been trying to make sense of it ever since. One year ago we had no idea how much we could hurt, how much we could endure, how kind people could be, how emotionally vulnerable we could be. I have hurt so much and learned so much. Life will never be the same; there is a big hole that will never be filled. So much has changed in my world and in me. And I miss Kym so badly it hurts. I am SO glad she was my daughter for thirty-one years."

When the second anniversary rolled around and still people remembered with emails, cards, calls, flowers on her grave, and personal expressions, Bill and I were amazed. Perhaps the fact that her death was still an unsolved murder kept those dates more firmly in the minds of people. Even when the case was eventually closed five years later, some friends did not forget. Four friends came to our house a few days later and planted a red maple tree in our yard in memory of Kym, a living tribute to her life and their compassion. Six years, seven years later a phone call or email from a friend who remembered the pain of that day meant more than words can ever express. For whatever reason, learning that someone else remembered was so very comforting to our family. And I learned something about the ministry of remembering!

> *Give thanks for those of your family who are still with you and know that your loved one remains with you in your memories.*
>
> Katherine O'Hara in *A Grief Like No Other: Surviving the Violent Death of Someone You Love*[49]

---

[49] O'Hara, 116

It Is Never Too Late

Other people's taking care of you, their understanding of your pain, and their belief that you can rebuild are the crossbeams that bear you up.

Barbara Rosof in *The Worst Loss: How Families Heal from the Death of a Child*[50]

On Mother's Day, nine months after Kym's death, a beautiful hydrangea arrived from a former classmate of our younger son, expressing her concern for us. What a lovely thing for her to do. When I called her mother, to ask for her address to thank her, I heard this story: Her daughter who now lived in another state, told her mother that she wanted to express her concern, but she had waited too long to do so. Her mother replied, "It is never too late." And I learned another lesson. She is so right. There is no such thing as expressing sympathy too late. Whenever it comes, it is most welcome. And "late" often comes when the mourner thinks no one cares any more.

---

[50] Rosof, 240

Long after the initial expressions of care had waned, here came a friend with a chicken from his grill, or a friend with chicken pie, or a co-worker with apple pie It is never too late. After I went back to work a colleague brought our supper one evening knowing that getting to work was a big effort and not much cooking would follow.

It really is never too late for expressions of care, a card, a call, a flower, a visit. Grief does not go away. It is never too late to care that another person has lost what cannot be replaced. There is no such thing as too late.

In the past I have chastised myself for failing to express my care in a timely manner. Sometimes I just did nothing because I thought it was too late or I was embarrassed that I had waited too long. Now I know my friend was right, it is never too late to let someone know I care.

It is never too late
Marilyn to Robin in 2005

To Dream Again

. . .two flawed assumptions: one, that life should always be fair; and two, that people (especially other people) get what they deserve. What seductive concepts these are!

Kathleen Brehony in *After the Darkest Hour: How Suffering Begins the Journey to Wisdom*[51]

As I walked on the beach almost three years after Kym's death, I reflected on my dreams. Like many other parents I suppose, I had dreamed of children growing up, marrying, having children, and bringing them all back home on occasions for happy times with children and grandchildren filling the house. Four children, four spouses, and a house full of grandchildren, would mean many happy times as family on holidays, at the beach, sitting around a large table. Of course we would have minor problems, but we would deal with those. The possibility of one of them getting a divorce had briefly crossed my mind, but down deep I thought it wouldn't happen to us. And I never even contemplated a death of a child.

---

[51] Brehony, 34

Those dreams were fractured twice when two of our children went through divorces. Divorced families can be mended, however. But our family was permanently broken when Kym died. Dreams were not only broken, but they were also shattered. We could not mend this change in our family. Ours is not the only family to have broken dreams. In fact, we had joined a host of families with shattered dreams. I look around me and see many families whose lives have not gone as they wished. Losses of various kinds of force families into new paths they do not choose.

Barbara Rosof speaks of the illusion that "the world is a safe and orderly place. Our family is especially safe. Nothing bad will happen to you. We, your parents, have the power to keep you safe.. . [these].illusions are essential to children's growing up whole. Before their own resources are sufficient to rely on, these essential illusions make it possible for children to feel safe. . .A child's death," she says, " tears the canopy [of illusions] wide open. Parents and siblings stand robbed of the child, bereft of their illusions, exposed, overwhelmed, alone."[52]

I kept reading Barbara Rosof. A psychotherapist who focused on working with parents who have lost a child, it seemed she was writing directly to me. "When your child dies, you lose simultaneously on so many fronts. You lose the embodiment of your special hopes, and you lose your second chance. You lose someone who loved you and whom you loved,

---

[52] Rosof, 1-2

perhaps more extravagantly than anyone else in your life. In your own eyes you have failed, because you could not protect your child. You lose a job and a piece of whom you know yourself to be. You are cheated of the natural order of time and generations. The tapestry of your future has been torn and forever altered." [53] Rosof knows how I feel. But I cannot get stuck there.

Some families seem to have their dreams realized and I am happy for them and the joy those dreams have brought them. Several years ago I would have told you that I would be envious of others who had joy I no longer had. Surprisingly to me, I have experienced few of those moments. Occasionally hearing the happy family stories of others is painful for me; but that is my problem, not theirs. Most often, seeing a happy family brings a smile to my face and warmth to my heart. That has been a surprise, and I cannot explain it. Perhaps it is one of God's many gifts to me.

Of course many families have to dream again. Ours was not the first and will not be the last. Families who deal with issues of health, divorce, job loss, death, fire, and flood have to dream again. In fact, there are likely few families whose dreams are realized as they first envisioned them.

As I reflected on all of this while walking down the sandy shore, I realized that my fractured dreams could

---

[53] Rosof, 19

be repaired. Were my dreams unrealistic? Should I have never dared to dream? No, dreaming is a natural, positive, optimistic way of thinking. Who dreams any other way? And why not? Perhaps they were the "happily ever after" unrealistic dreams to begin with. But I make no apologies about having them.

Now I knew I needed new dreams. These dreams would have new dimensions. I dream of wisdom, strength, peace, being family through thick and thin. Happiness is redefined as are dreams. For 65 years I was a very fortunate person to have a happy life and family with few problems or crises. Sixty-five years of a rather rosy life with many rosy dreams realized. In many ways I am a fortunate woman who has lived a blessed life. For that I am most grateful. Many people are not so fortunate. Now I had the opportunity to learn and grow from brokenness, loss, and pain. Now I could learn how to be more compassionate. Now I would go deeper into my own soul. Now I am a different person with different dreams. I dream again, but more realistic dreams. Dreams now have more depth, are less superficial.

Some of my reading was helpful as I re-dreamed. The first book I read was Kathleen Brehony's *After the Darkest Hour*. I couldn't imagine having an hour much darker than I was having so this seemed like a good book for me to read. Brehony knows that there are many circumstances in life that can lead to our darkest hour. Death of a loved one is one of those. She says that the "dark night of the soul. . .[is where] we are stripped bare of our previously held illusions and our insistence on seeing life as we would like it to be rather than as it is."[54] Well, that is exactly where I found myself.

Brook Noel and Pamela Blair assured me that ". . .this shattering of assumptions is necessary in grief. We must re-evaluate what we once held as true, move through the ruin and create a new foundation based on what we have learned."[55] Later they add, ". . .the question becomes, Now What? After expecting life to take a certain course, it has chosen its own, far from your plan."[56] As I walked down by the seashore I was beginning to wrestle with that Now What question.

I needed to re-dream. New dreams are shaped differently, perhaps more realistically. Looking forward with a new configuration of family was a necessary part of moving on. A word of caution from Brehony helped me get some emotional footing: "So many of us so often forgo the present moment for memories of the past or expectations of the future." [57] Dwelling in the past is not healthy. Getting stuck in the "what ifs" is not healthy. Expecting a fairy-like future is not healthy. I must not "forgo the present moment." The present is the one reality I have. I cannot change the past. I do not know the future. I will take it one day at a time and dream. Optimism about the future is the attitude that fits me. I dream

---

[54] Brehony, 48

[55] Noel and Blair, 38

[56] Noel and Blair, 41

[57] Brehony, 190

that our lives will be good, whatever that will mean in a given year.

I do dream again but dream differently: I have fewer set patterns and many more question marks. My dreams are not as rosy; I make fewer assumptions. I don't project as far with my dreams. Some dreams as "as is" dreams. As Brehony says "our preoccupation with trying to control the future is a great source of suffering."[58]

Happiness is intrinsic. I learned a long time ago, but I have had to relearn it. Internal happiness must be my core. Any other happiness is icing on the cake. I still believe in optimistic, positive dreaming, knowing now that I can adjust if and when it is necessary. The years 2002-2004 significantly rearranged my dreams and taught me much. That's life. Grace has brought me here so far and grace will lead me on, to paraphrase a popular hymn.

Dreams can be reborn.

> *Violence takes the future and destroys it—but. . .you [can] take back the future and make it yours again.*
>
> Kathleen O'Hara in *A Grief Like No Other: Surviving the Violent Death of Someone You Love* [59]

---

[58] Brehony, 191

[59] O'Hara, 174

What Do I Do with Forgiveness?

Be kind to one another, tenderhearted, forgiving one another, as God in Christ has forgiven you.

Ephesians 4:32

Kym was gone. I could not change that. Unlike her, my life was not taken, but it was permanently altered. One of the first ways it was altered was in my thinking about many, many things such as loss, death, life, family, and forgiveness.

Forgiveness! I am a Christian. I believe in forgiveness. There have been times in my life when I struggled with forgiveness. In fact, there was a time that I could not honestly say "and forgive us our trespasses as we forgive those who trespass against us." I simply could not get the words out of my mouth. I believe in forgiveness. But believing in it and practicing it are not the same.

As I began to climb out of my pit of numbness, I realized I had to deal with forgiveness. As a person who takes the teachings of Jesus seriously I knew that I should forgive. But *should* and *would* were two very different paths. I wanted to forgive the man who stole Kym's life because it was the Christian thing to do. But I could not. My motive to work on forgiveness was not what I had hoped.

I talked to God about my struggle again and again as I walked. "God, I want to forgive because it is the Christian thing to do, but to be honest that is not motivating me right now. I am ashamed to admit it, God, but I want to forgive right now for selfish reasons. I do not want to be a bitter woman the rest of my life. He took Kym's life. I do not want to let him control my emotions for the rest of my life. I am being selfish, God. I do not want bitterness to envelop me, so I have to forgive and free myself. God, I thought I was a better Christian than this, but I am not. So there it is. For now, help me to forgive – selfishly." I was ashamed of that prayer, but I prayed dozens of times. It may be the most honest prayer I have ever uttered.

Selfishness drove my pursuit of forgiveness.
I was not proud of this attitude of self-centeredness. I *wanted* to forgive because I believed as a Christian that it was the right attitude to have. But down deep I knew that I really wanted to forgive to be free of hate and anger. It is like C.S. Lewis said: "Everyone says that forgiveness is a lovely idea, until they have something to forgive." [60] That lovely idea did not

---

[60] As quoted in Behoney, 185

sound so lovely to me. How could I be lovely in the midst of such horror?

Yet when I thought about the years ahead of me I simply did not want to live them in bitterness and anger. All of the bitterness and anger my body, mind, and soul could express would never bring Kym back. So what was its value? I wanted to live a life of as much peace as I could get. In order to do that, I *had* to forgive. For *my* sake I had to forgive. If I wanted peace, there was no other option. Whether or not I forgave the person who took Kym's life would impact every day I lived and might have absolutely no impact at all on her killer. So if I did not forgive I would pay the heaviest penalty.

Coming to that conclusion added another kind of pain for I wanted to think that I would do what a Christian should do for noble reasons. But I was choosing this path because it made me feel better. That was not the image of myself I wanted to have. But there it was. As I walked I admitted to myself that this motive was the best I could do at this time. Perhaps later I could be noble.

Forgiving is letting go
Imagine my relief months later when I was reminded in Lewis Smede's *The Art of Forgiving* that forgiveness is for one's self. In fact forgiveness is turning loose or letting go of those harsh feelings that imprison us. Then I remembered the memorial service we had for Kym. Art and Alan wanted their friend and Kym's to sing and play the guitar at her service. They asked him to play something Kym would like. At her service he

played and sang a Beatles piece, apologizing that he could not find an appropriate Duran Duran piece since that was her favorite. So he sang "Let It Be." "Whisper words of wisdom, let it be." Although I was too emotionally fried at that time to get the significance of that song for my journey, I heard "let it be" within days of the tragedy. I can't change the terrible things that happen. I only have the power to change how I respond to the painful things that happen to me. I have to let it be.

What forgiveness is not
Books on forgiveness begin to line my shelf. As I read I learned so much more about forgiveness. Forgiving another does not mean you are condoning or excusing what he or she does. It does not necessarily lead to reconciling with that person. Forgiving certainly does not relieve the other person of the responsibility of dealing with the brokenness she or he has caused. Forgiveness does not mean forgetting. Learning all of that was very helpful. Sorting out what forgiveness was and was not brought clarity to my struggle with forgiveness.

The benefits of a forgiving attitude were very attractive to me. Revenge, bitterness, anger, and hatred would poison the very core of my being. If I could forgive I would push those destructive feelings out, leaving room for more healthy feelings. I want peace. Bitterness and peace cannot live in the same house. The gift of turning loose of those hateful feelings was peace. Poison or peace? I chose peace.

Discovering grace

Of course, peace is not accomplished by one day making that decision. Forgiveness is an ongoing challenge. But I have learned that it feels so much better to forgive than it does to refuse to do so. It is still a selfish thing for me. I believe Jesus taught it because he knew it was so good for the offended as well as the offender. To be forgiven is grace. To be able to forgive is grace also. A key resource in my journey of forgiveness was Philip Yancy's *What's So Amazing About Grace*. Yancy challenged me to know grace at a new level.

One more word about forgiveness. One of my biggest challenges as I have already mentioned is forgiving myself. At times I had the irrational idea that if only I had been with Kym she would not have been killed. But of course I did not live with her so why would I have popped in that night? That crazy idea would not rattle around in my head very often. But it did keep recurring.

The greater forgiveness issue I had was forgiving myself for not being more "with it" as my mother came to the end of her journey. I still have moments when I am hard on myself for not being with her when she died. I was still taking sleeping pills after Kym's death, so I was sleeping soundly at 4:30 AM when that call came telling me of Mother's death. The sitter was holding her hand when she died, not me. I have to tell myself again the futility of that attitude and the benefits of forgiving myself.

The peace of forgiving is not perfect. That peace is interrupted when those poisonous feelings erupt once in a while. The work of forgiving is ongoing. And worth every effort.

> *And forgive us our trespasses, as we forgive those who trespass against us.*
> Matthew 6:12

What is Justice?

The story of how your loved [one] died is one that will stay with you forever. It may dominate your life for a long time, maybe for the rest of your life.. . .It will reconstruct and change as times change, and hopefully it will contain humor and good things, too.

Kathleen O'Hara in *A Grief Like No Other: Surviving the Violent Death of Someone You Love*[61]

One of the things we were thankful for from the first day of this journey was that the authorities we dealt with seemed to be very caring people. As it turned out, one of the policemen immediately on the scene had gone to school with Kym as had one of the detectives who worked on the case. That some of the officials had a personal interest in the case helped our

---

[61] O'Hara, 2

107

confidence. Small towns have an advantage at times like this.

However, from the beginning others who had traveled a similar path warned us of the frustrations of working with the justice system. After all a legal system is not the same as a justice system. We got letters from strangers who expressed their sympathy and support as we dealt with the courts. And what is justice after all? It is getting Kym back; that is justice to us. But that cannot be.

Since a suspect was identified within a matter of weeks, I was sure that within a few months we would be in court, and it would all be over. (I had watched too many law and order programs on TV where the cases are solved in an hour!) Because the evidence was largely circumstantial, the case was not quickly solved. In fact, it was five years and one month before we heard the guilty plea and sentence. It was a wait I never imagined and never wanted. However, five years gave me a lot of time to sort through some emotions.

The long wait

Had the case gone to court within a year, it would have been more difficult for me emotionally, for I was so very emotionally raw and fragile at that time. Five years gave me the ability to go to court with more emotional strength. During those five years was it disturbing to have an indictment, but no court date? Yes. Was it disappointing, to put it mildly, when we went to court several times only to have another delay? Oh, yes. Was it stressful to keep wondering if the suspect would ever really be punished? You bet!

The authorities kept reassuring us that the procedure was for the best and we believed them because we wanted to. But the days, weeks, months, and years kept ticking by.

With less than twenty-four hours' notice we learned that he would be in court to plead guilty. We were there! We heard the plea and the sentence. But it did not feel like I thought it would. Perhaps I thought it would be relief and finality and that would feel good. Instead my emotions tanked again that day. I felt as low and sad and grieved as I had felt in the weeks immediately after Kym's death. That surprised me. A friend called that day and noticed the sadness in my voice. She expressed her concern. I told her that I thought a good night's rest would put me back on track and it did. But I was taken back by the emotional response to that long-awaited day. My cousin who years earlier had suffered a similar tragedy, put it well a few days later. She said the feeling was hollow and like a funeral. Hollow and funeral. Those words nailed the feeling precisely. I guess this was justice, but it didn't feel good like I had hoped.

This journey revealed several surprises about myself, positive and negative, as I have already mentioned. Perhaps the biggest dealt with capital punishment.

Capital punishment

For over twenty years I team-taught with a political science professor, a class on church and state issues. Each time we addressed the topic of capital punishment I said, "I do not believe in capital punishment. If people should not kill, neither should the state. However, I am sure if someone in my family is ever killed, I will want that person put to death as punishment. It is the job of the state to protect that person from my vengeance." At least twenty times I made that public statement. Every word was so very honest.

Yet not once since Kym was murdered have I wanted the suspect to be put to death. And for a reason I had never dreamed of. The very thought of taking the life of another mother's child is simply unbearable to me now. How could I *ever* do that to another woman? To my surprise I was not thinking about the suspect, but about his family. The principle of no capital punishment is still important to me, but that is not what shapes my stance now. My own deep loss and grief has been so profound that there is absolutely no woman I would want to experience it if I could prevent it. Surprise, surprise again. Repeatedly I learned I did not know myself as well as I thought.

Several trips to court rooms gave me a new insight. There are victims on both sides of court room. As I saw the suspect's family members sit through some of those sessions, I thought of the pain they must be experiencing. What must it feel like to sit in court and watch your child or sibling charged with murder? Oh my, I never want to know what that feels like.

Now I read or hear the news differently. Every person who is murdered is someone's child. Unless that parent is dead, that parent is on the journey one must travel when a child dies. There is a lot of pain behind the headlines.

Wanting to know

Every family member is different in his or her response to loss. We discovered that on many occasions. I have been at odds with my family when it came to getting information. All of us were eager to hear what the authorities could tell us. But I wanted other information. I wanted to see the autopsy report. My family could not understand why. The detective on the case provided me with a copy. That was one more piece of information in the puzzlement of Kym's death. I knew a little bit more about her death.

I wanted to know everything that anyone else knew about her last moments on earth. I wanted to see all of the evidence. I didn't want anyone to know something I didn't know.

The Assistant District Attorney and the Tennessee Bureau of Investigation detective told me that I would eventually have access to that. Bill, Art, and Alan argued vigorously, and I mean vigorously, that I should not go there. They pleaded and begged. Although Art was calling from Denver, you could almost feel him on his knees begging, he was so determined that I do not see the evidence. He did not want me to see the photos made after her death. I argued just as vigorously that I appreciated their concern and care, that it was my decision, not theirs. Yes, I might regret it, but I was willing to live with that. I had two overriding concerns: I wanted answers. I can live with periods better than question marks when it comes to matters such as this. I wanted to know everything those authorities knew about my daughter's death. I was her mother after all. They should not know more than I did, I thought.

In the meantime, I read with great relief that Barbara Rosof, who had worked with many grieving parents understood. She said, "The search for facts is in part a search for your child as he was and will never be again. At once a holding on and a letting go,. . . [it] may be the first step toward building a new reality, toward learning how to live a life without your child."[62] Now I had expert support for my decision.

Brook Noel and Pamela D. Blair gave me more support: "Our mind will look for the beginning (What happened?) the middle (How did he/she feel, respond, progress?), the end (Was he in pain? Did he have any last thoughts or words?) . . .In order to get to a place where we can think about the experience in its entirety, we must know as much of the cycle as possible.. . .As our questions lessen, we create more room to heal."[63] I was determined to get as much information as I could. Now I had more confidence that it was the right thing for me to do. This quest could give me more room to heal.

Almost six years after Kym's death, the detective and I made arrangements for me to see the evidence. For three hours he sat in our living room and went over photos, transcripts of testimonies, and other

---

[62] Rosof, 200

[63] Noel and Blair, 43

information in his two boxes of files. Many questions were answered. Many pieces began to fit together. It was not an easy revisiting of that horrible night, but it was an informative one. Ten months later I sat in the Assistant District Attorney's office, examining her files on this case. More pieces put into place. I have a better understanding of what happened to Kym on that horrible night in August of 2004 and what the authorities have done to solve the case.

Since I cannot have Kym back, at least I can know as much as possible of her last moments. The knowledge of those moments brings a lot of pain. But my journey since that tragedy has been made with the help of family, many caring friends, and a loving God. The pain is less sharp. The peace is more constant.

> *What you do not know you cannot lay to rest.*
>
> Barbara Rosof in *The Worst Loss: How Families Heal from the Death of a Child*[64]

---

[64] Rosof, 209

Gift

A beauty unique One of God's best. . .
Made in His image But with her own style. .
. Only one life- But she lived it her way. .
.Only one life- But nothing's worth more.

Hank Niceley in a tribute to Kym[65]

The journey of pain that began with Kym's tragic death left a trail of gifts on its path. Although I did not want to walk this way, I have learned so much. Writing this story was a way of working through the pain and remembering what I have learned. I am not the same person today that I was the day before Kym died. I hope I am a better me.

On a hot July day in 1973 a charming 15-month-old girl came off that Northwest plane and into our

---

[65] Hank Niceley, *Only One Life*, 2004

family's arms. What a gift we had for the next 31 years.

A toddler who raced down the driveway in her big wheel

A Pre-schooler who cut her own hair, letting us know what a fine hairdresser she would be as she got older

The "do-it-myself" 3-year-old who insisted on tying her own shoes
The fourth grader who made a poor grade in reading because she "couldn't get her mind off of John Snyder" in Dukes of Hazard

The middle-schooler who insisted on wearing neon-colored clothes

The teen-ager who loved to read

The young woman with good penmanship who did beautiful calligraphy

The college student who had a good time for three years, then returned as a non-traditional student who did very well

A young woman who loved to travel

A young adult with a good business head on her shoulders

A doting aunt

A person who loved pigs, and red, and books, and her Honda

How rich we are to have had her as a daughter. Although she no longer lives in her body, she thrives in our memories. Every time someone mentions her name, it is another gift delivered.

Aren't we blessed!

> *Grieving is not a short-term process; it's not even a long-term process; it's a lifelong process. .. . . [it] does not have a final event built into it. . . grievers [who transcend] come to recognize the loss as a watershed event in their lives, as a meaningful life turning point.*[66]

"A deep distress hath humanized my soul"
William Wordsworth

---

[66] Ashley Davis Prend, Transcending Loss: Understanding the Lifelong Impact of Grief and How to Make it Meaningful, (New York: Berkley, 1997) xv, 55, 85

Acknowledgements

One of the reasons for writing this story was to remember the many kind deeds and the many kind friends who ministered to me and my family on this journey. One of the reasons for publishing this story is to publicly acknowledge the significance of their acts of kindness. An earlier version was full of the names of those folks. Then I discovered that the names at times distracted from their acts. The reader might be trying to figure out who the person was rather than focusing on the deed. I hope that reading this story might be helpful to the reader who is looking for ways to reach out to others in times of loss.

The people who have walked with us on this journey are too numerous to mention in one story. Some cared in ways too deep to be conveyed in this narrative. Many people whose acts appear in these pages are not people whom we knew well, and who surprised us with their attention and care. For every person who reached out to us in the last seven and a half years we are so grateful. Only God knows how much that has meant to us and what each person has taught us about caring.

In appreciation to the ones whose stories I have told I share their names here: Marilyn Barr, Cathy Brown, Pat Brown, Mark Brown, Debbie Coyle, Jim Dampier, Don Garner, Sheryl Gray, Robin Barr Geurs, Nancy Harper, Melissa Hensley, Monty

Jordan, Brenda Lanning, Travis Lanning, Beverly McClellan, Barbara McDougal, Clark Measels, Nenette Measels, Hank Niceley, David Nowell, Joy Powell, Cheryl Prose, Scott Seal, Bob Shurden, Buddy Shurden, Irene Shurden, Kay Shurden, Val Silver, Brenda Sloan, Joe Bill Sloan, Lynn Taylor, Susan Underwood, Juanita Vanaman, Beth Van Landingham, Gene Wilder, and John Zirkle. Thanks to Martha Bill Weierman (deceased) for teaching me that "fine" can be redefined. A special thanks to Nenette Measels who carefully proofread this story, a tedious task so well done. Since that proofing I have tinkered with the story a time or two so any errors now are mine, not hers.

Writing this story was a very private enterprise. No one knew I was writing it, not even my family. They knew I was keeping a journal but did not know I was writing a separate account of my grieving process. About a year ago I told Bill what I was doing. Last fall I told our children. Early this year I sent each of them a copy and asked for their feedback. I knew it was a heavy request, but they all agreed to read it and respond.

Suzanne, whose edict prompted Kym's arrival in our family, Art and Alan who discovered her departure, have supported this effort although it carried them back through some painful memories. In many ways my story is their story. I am deeply grateful for each of them. Bill has been my daily partner on this trip of pain and peace. Without his support and encouragement this book would not have been a reality. I do not know how I would have made the journey of grief or the task of making this story public without him.

Most of all, I am grateful for Kym who gifted our family with 31 years of being a curious pre-schooler, challenging grade-schooler, a typical teen-ager, delightful young adult, and fascinating woman.

April 2012

Works Cited

Brehony, Kathleen A. *After the Darkest Hour: How Suffering Begins the Journey to Wisdom.* (Henry Holt & Co., 2000).

Holy Bible, *New Revised Standard Version.* (Harper Collins Publishers), 2008.

Niceley, Hank. *Only One Life.* 2004.

Noel, Brook and Pamela D. Blair. *I Wasn't Ready to Say Goodbye: Surviving, Coping and Healing After the Sudden Death of a Loved One.* (Champion Press, 2000).

O'Hara, Kathleen. *A Grief Like No Other: Surviving the Violent Death of Someone You Love.* (Marlowe & Co., 2006).

Prend, Ashley Davis. *Transcending Loss: Understanding the Lifelong Impact of Grief and How to Make It Meaningful.* (Berkley Books, 1997).

Rosof, Barbara D. *The Worst Loss: How Families Heal from the Death of A Child.*(Henry Holt& Co., 1994)

www.ingramcontent.com/pod-product-compliance
Lightning Source LLC
Chambersburg PA
CBHW060244030426
42335CB00014B/1591